Entomology

poetic musings on love

McKayla Grace

ISBN: 978-0-578-78200-3

Dedication

for those
who took their ebony strands
and entangled my soul
with ocean depths and florescent eyes
with velvet wings and murky lips
drenching clouds with their ecstasy and their
treachery.

This is Entomology.

Lampyridae's

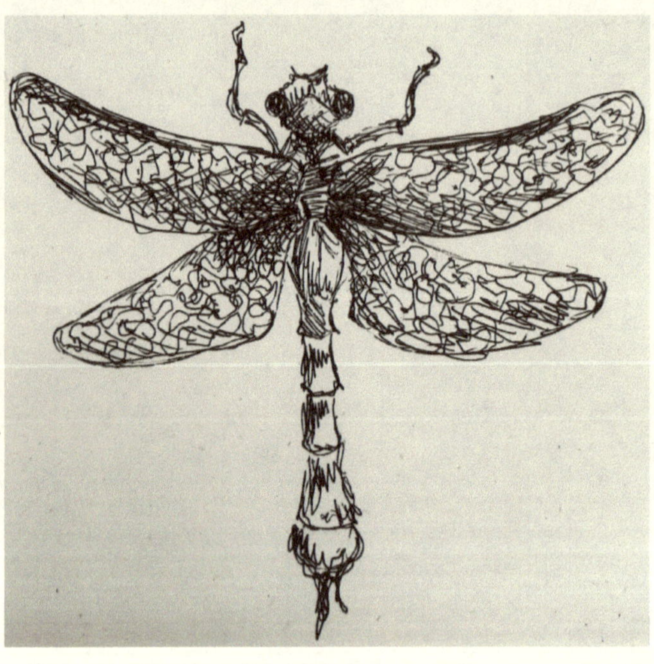

The flavor of my name

does it blossom the honeydew evenings
of our August nights?
or does it sit heavily
upon his throat?
the mud of love and unrequited passions
in those daffodil dusks?
does he ponder it as maroon flamboyance of desert clay?
or is its beautiful squalor
too heavenly for his curious purple mouth?

The summer of butterfly searchlights

seaweed stuck to feet, like slivered golden veins.
sharp cedar clung to stars, in heavy earthy nights.
it was here, we filled our brains
lounging in sugar coated grass.
and dared to dream and talk of love,
among other things that would never be.

Confess

if i left you today,
would your heart lay out?
watering roses,
fragrant. coppery.
or would you tear away our pages
crumbling tightly bundled words
drifting. fading. smoke.
is our love your breath?
or is it just a crutch.

But earth gives life

i treated your sorry ass
LIKE
A
KING.
and in return?
you trampled me
like hideous dirt.

September

you gathered every strand
glinting in the autumn mist
within your icy grasp.
your laughter, stars of hell
tearing stitches from the soul you broke
and my agony,
lined your brain with gold.

You were my god complex

you tore away my angel wings like silk.
now i sit, stranded upon the earth
while you're in search of someone else

And yet you broke me

your mouth was done, spilling poison in my brain
And i felt vast seas
and saltwater.
but it could no longer heal
your hatred stings.
and they ruptured.
spilling flames of frenzy from my fists.

Entomology

Anthophila's

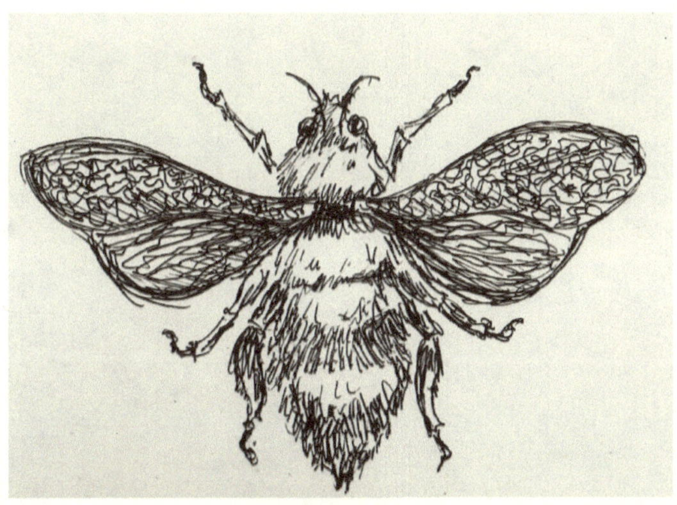

Rebound

tear the seams
once more, anthophila.
and purify my aching soul
with your
oh, so sweet
honey words.

I promise I'm dangerous...

he reminds me of saffron,
vibrant soul with subtle tastes.
the tickling tenderness
of a golden flame.
and so tonight i kissed another soul.
my lust
freely steaming into icy air.
what his silenced shivers couldn't know,
is that lava scorches earth to dust.
hope the seconds weren't enough
to spread eruptions to his core.
pray.
my magma
doesn't leave a firefly's blackened scar.

Idolization

i want to know
would it be so bad,
to strip these fabrics
bloodied by my burning hands?
to let the rain drench us
in the beauty
seen through each other's eyes?
and he answered,
picking the flowers of his soul
fashioning me a crown
glistening with dew,
declaring me his world.

Rejuvenation

his hands traced maps of jade
his mouth billowed white winters
his tongue brought monsoons as i let him enter,
oh, sweet cherry dusk.
Where his eyes met mine,
blossoming sensual secrets,
from his opened soul.

Solace

some nights my mind sprouts roots
that break through cranium like silt.
nourishing my starless dreams
with
royal romance flowers
velvet tongues
flowing golden hair
and the roses,
That shatter into eyes as your winter engulfs me.

Memory

i wore it all last night.
swung around my body
the same way you would hold me tight.
the faint scent of you
mixing with a salty breeze
i held my breath, letting you soak
into
my mouth
my nose
my memories
until the rugged gusts, whisked you up tossing you
into that shining morning sea.

Fantasy.

your eyes danced with the moon
and your open, airy, big sky laugh tickled my breasts
While your fingers brought me to my knees in awe.
i ran my wet kisses down like gentle rain
through the canyon crevice of your back.
your sun filled voice, tumbled waves upon heated island shores
as we devoured
every scrumptious memory
left within our grasp.

Anatomical

i wish,
i could see your cranium
your ligaments
your muscles
your heart
your lungs
so then, i would know
your actions
were human
and not the anthophila
i saw
within your mouth.

Stung

Lesson

i will write
about you in my pages
of the honey and the stings,
of the infidelity and the lust.
until you
no longer leave thorns upon my velvet tongue.
these words i pour not praise of your raindrop wings.
no, oh no, anthophila.
this is me
on how to respect the mountains in my soul
where you,
no longer soar.

Him.

that's it.
he's the poem
i could never write.

Ocean Dreams

we took the things
we cherished:
sea glass in our hands.
but the sand fractured
our eyes
our mouths
our breaths.
and those microscopic slices
seeped the forgotten love that whispered
"some things, my darling, are better left apart"

Honey words

your words: poisoned honey
suckled me for far too long.
please:
just leave me alone
so i can rise.
and you: can finally grasp
the edge of all your lies.

Proselytism

your words have become the lava
i feared would be my own,
and the facade that makes me hold you
to
my arms
my legs
my chest
my hips
my lips
disperses
as glowing rivers turn to ash.

Perception

no matter how desperate the soul is
to etch those sunsets into love
the ebony ink of night is bound to spread
the stands of flames will frizzle out
and the contrast of night and day
becomes the chaos of love itself.

Here lies…

today, i awoke.
my hands: bloody
my shovel: hit 6 feet.
i saw asphyxiation in your tomb of lust.
so, i flew to the sun
my angel wings soaked in gold
and the rays
finally tore your honeycomb stitches
from my standing soul.

Cicadoidea's

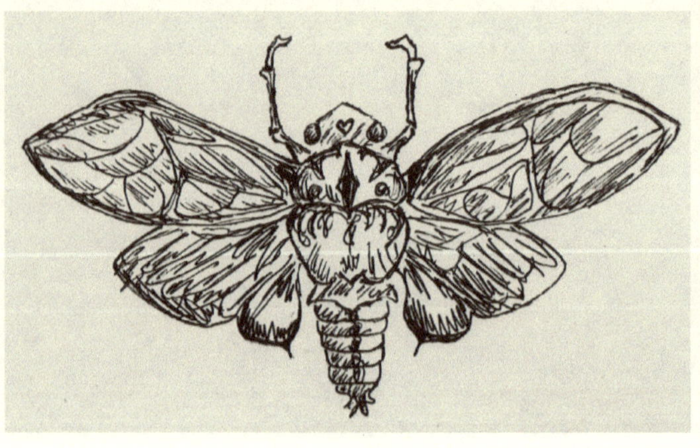

Sunday worship.

you touch every bee sting left inside me.
your nectar
healing every scar
my valley curves: your temple.
my flowing hair: your rivers
and my bones shattered to millions
with your tsunami touch.

Voracity

he wants to know me
like the rain knows the pavement
in this city of downpours.

Benediction

you yearn to continue your
worship
in my temple
in my rivers
and sing your hymns into every corner
until i believe there is such a place
as heaven
in this broken world.

Veneration

do I know the whispers of the rivers to the trees?
or is all this earth within me,
the ache for whispered words, and silken sheets?
is it my skin rattling and my bones raising,
those smooth corners of your sea glass eyes,
the mossy glow of mine?
is it the nebulas within your hands,
your lips and tongue whispering to mine
that dusk and dawn
are portraits
and time has no place with love
and love, no place with time?

Through my eyes

i am the girl who worships
the murder of the crows.
those million shades of
prussian blue,
feathers of the sky.
where galaxies birthed
a night, glittering with diamonds
and the music of your eyelashes
serenaded robins
and the golden moon.

I Am Enough

midnight as we lay entangled in ocean sheets
your hands. my body.
the earthquakes, in rivers, crept and flowed
and my eyelashes sighed
as your devotion traced the body i once despised.
your fingers, skinny dipped in my pools of twilight.
my sharpened lips
held you to my quivering body
and let the wind whisper across our skin.
singing my love into delighted ears
as my confidence oozed into that elated night.

Golden hour

you are the moon
and i a field of daisies,
fluttering back petals
to your blankets of lunar rubies.
and the birds called your kisses
across my thighs and into my valleys and my roots.
sinking into the twilight
your tongue spread across my brain.

You wanted

to wrap your hands
your fingers
your whispers
through my curves.
to taste the daffodil sugar
that lay dusted upon my breasts,
the moonshine across my lips.

you wanted my skin
my folds
my sultry glances.
to watch my vibrant shadows
dance across my bedroom walls
As you became my one AM addiction

Serenity

i do not know how
to braid my own hair.
so, i will ask you,
with thick butter of embarrassment in my throat,
to weave my wild into your splendored smile.
to swallow my lavender skies.
to murmur my thirst for adventure into life.
to pluck the fruits from my locks
and let the sweet sticky juice of memories
trickle down your tongue.
to divulge in delicious imperfections
and welcome them within your heart.

Treachery

i found you in my august nights,
and brought you to a long-lost land
where the sun sang truths of life.
and you took my glorious ocean scars,
and gathered my sweetened dusk,
forged them into a glinting sword.
and the blade
banished me from my own paradise.
and those beautiful words i wrote,
sat crumpled in the dust.
and here they turned into smoke and flames and i learned
our love was really just your crutch.

Mantodea

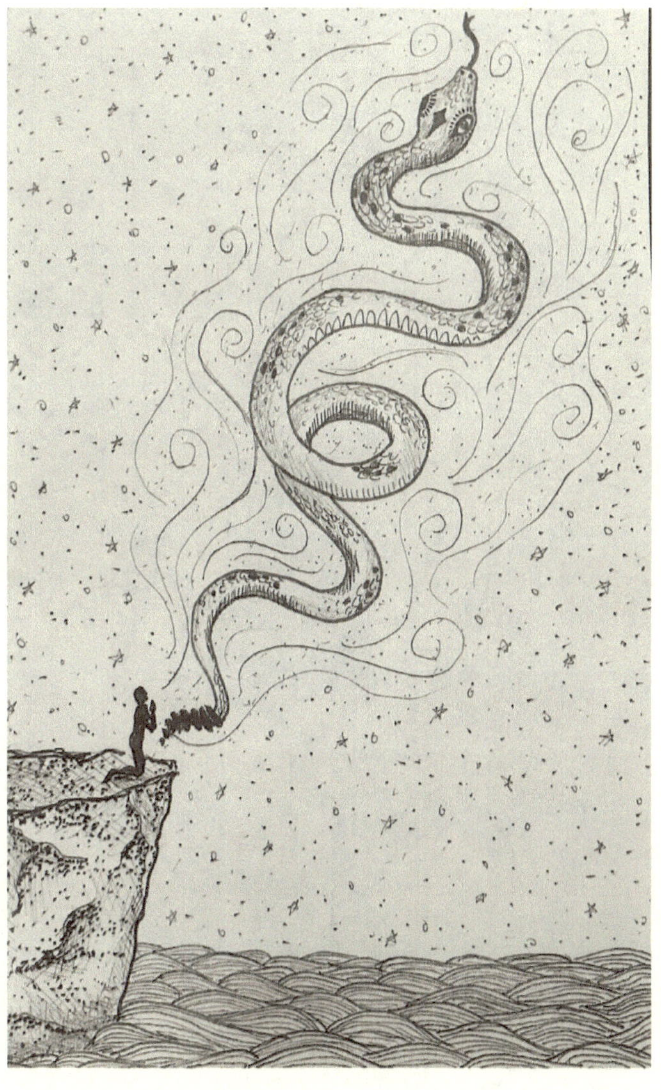

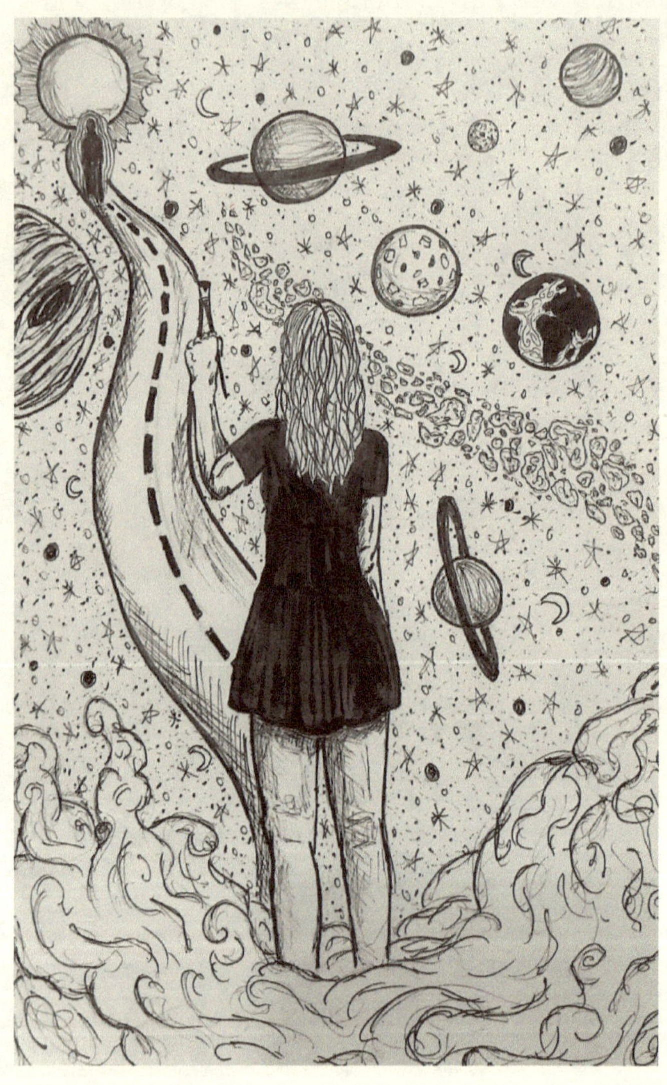

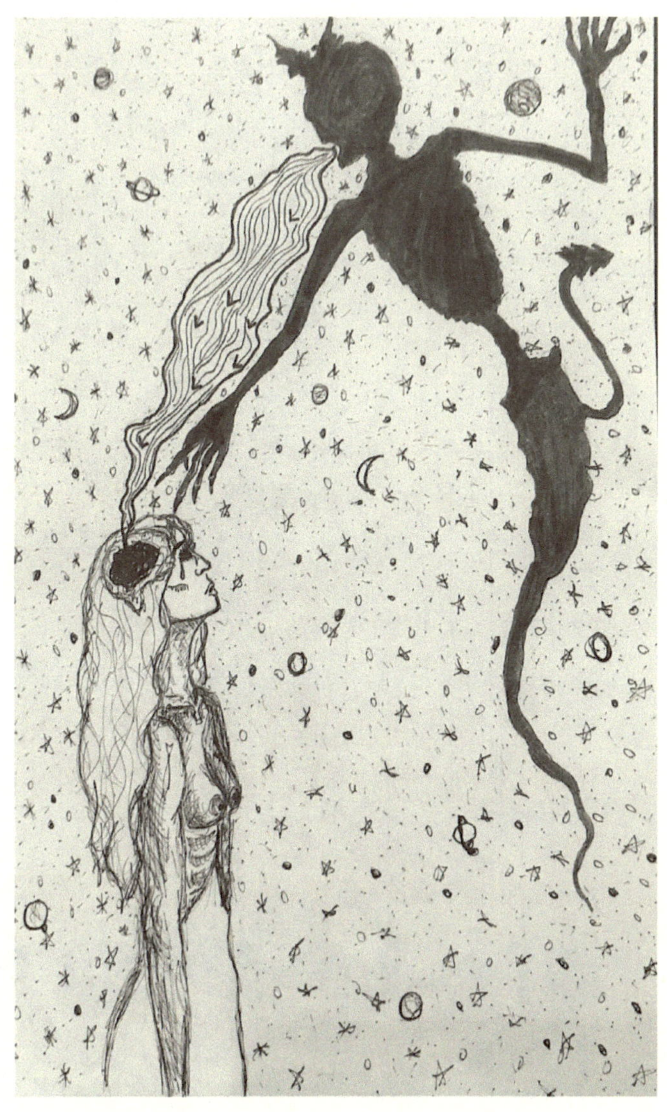

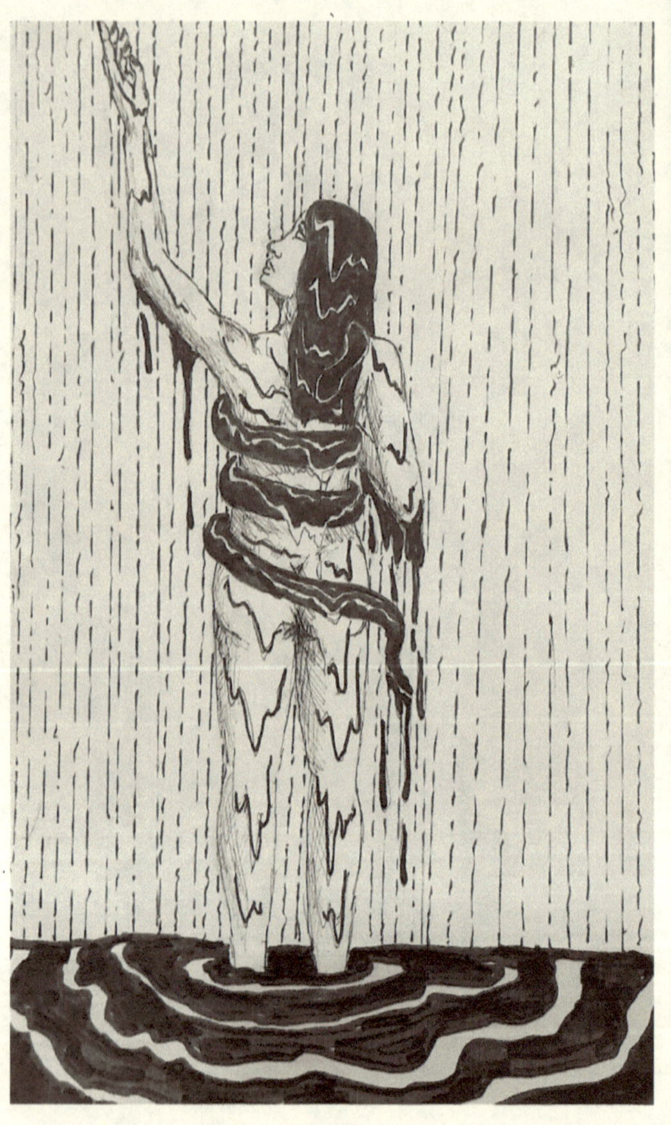

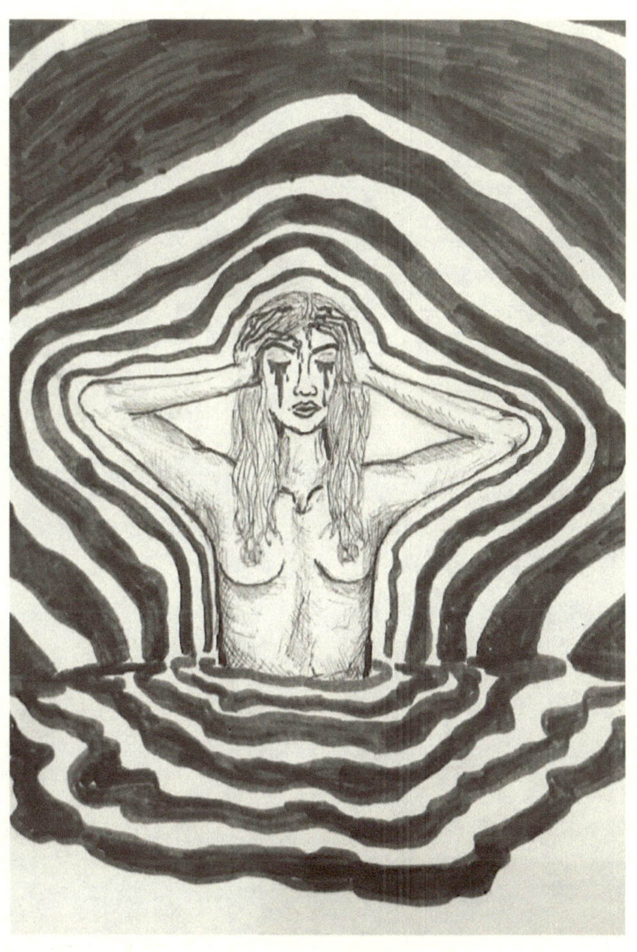

Entomology

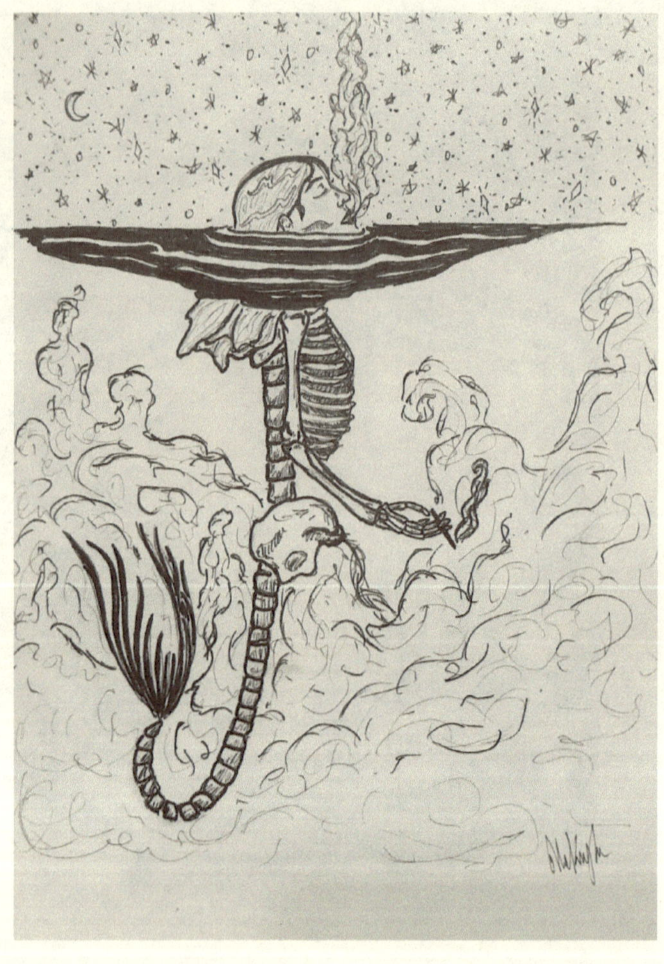

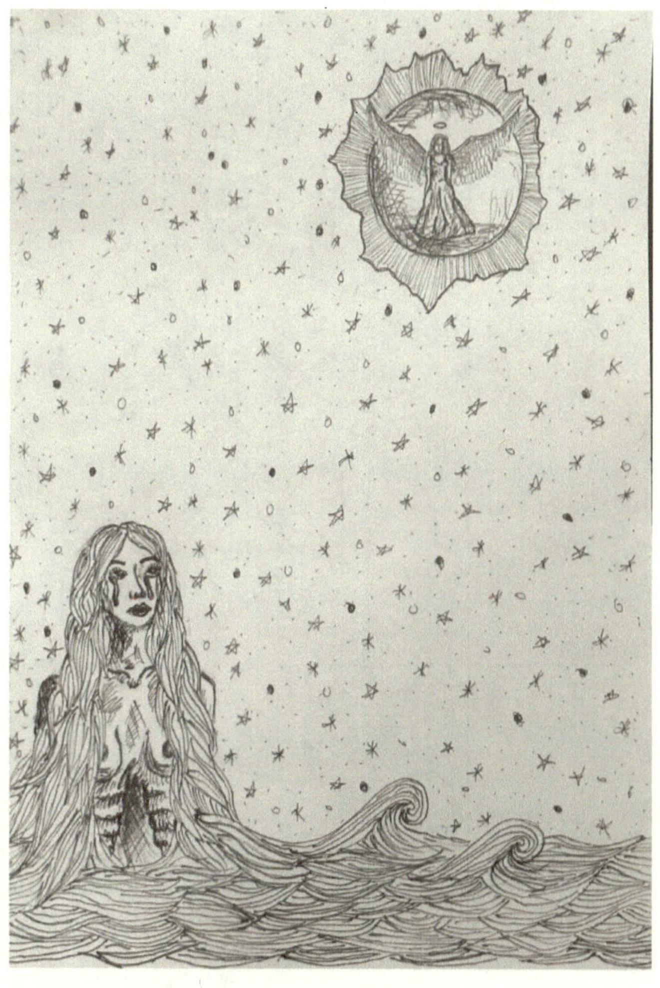

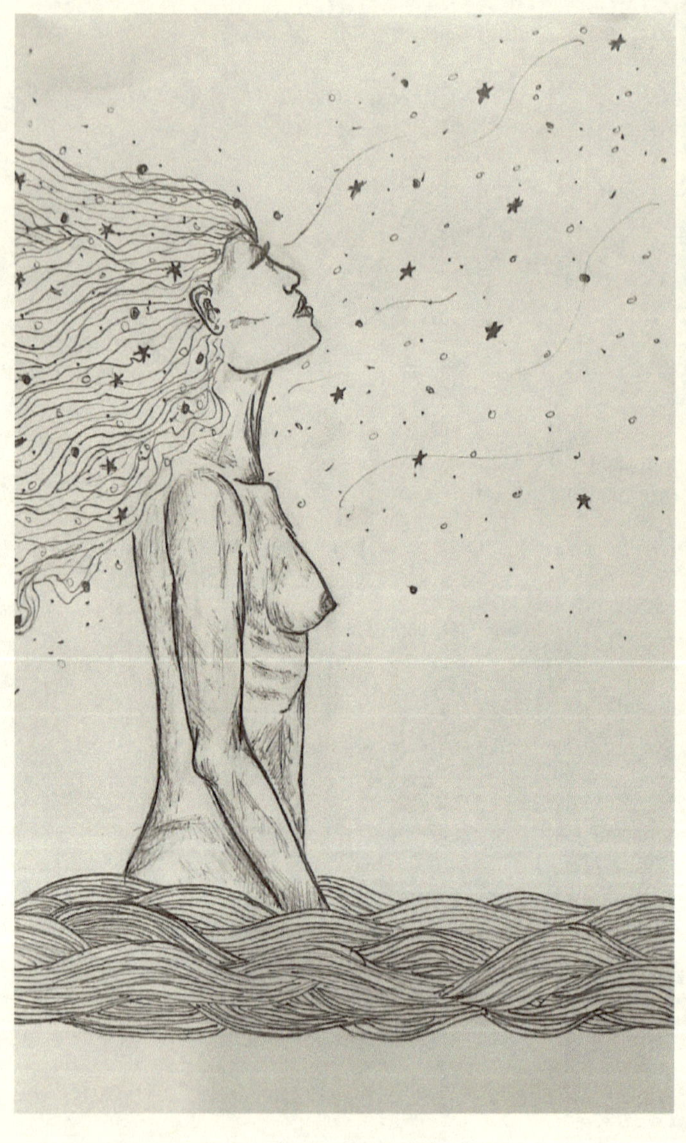

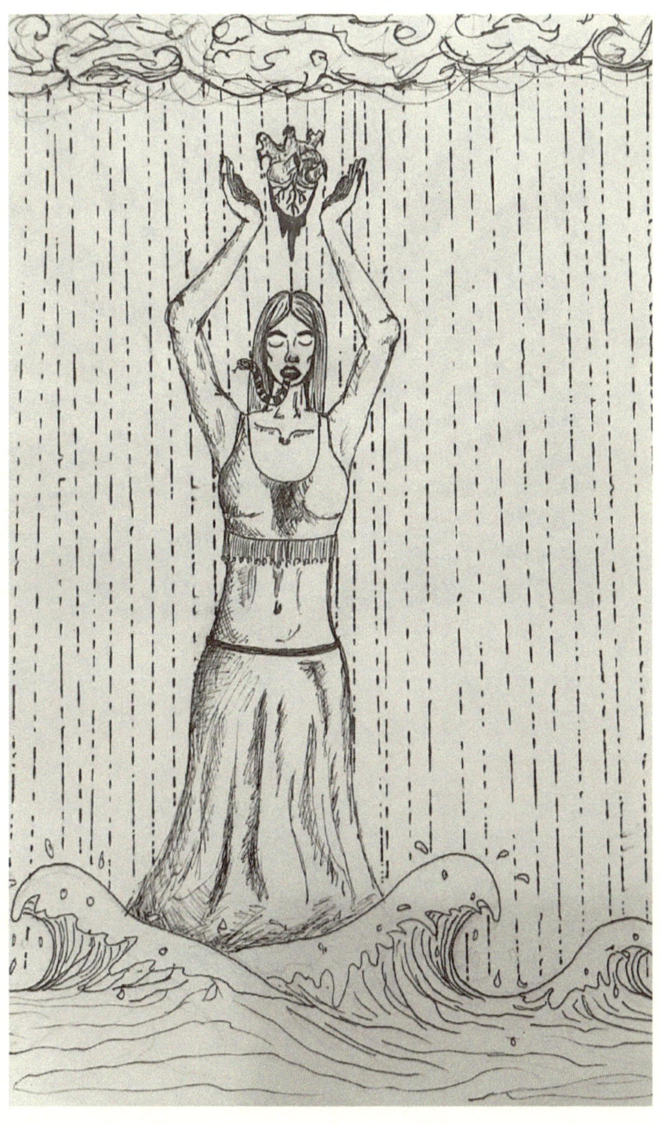

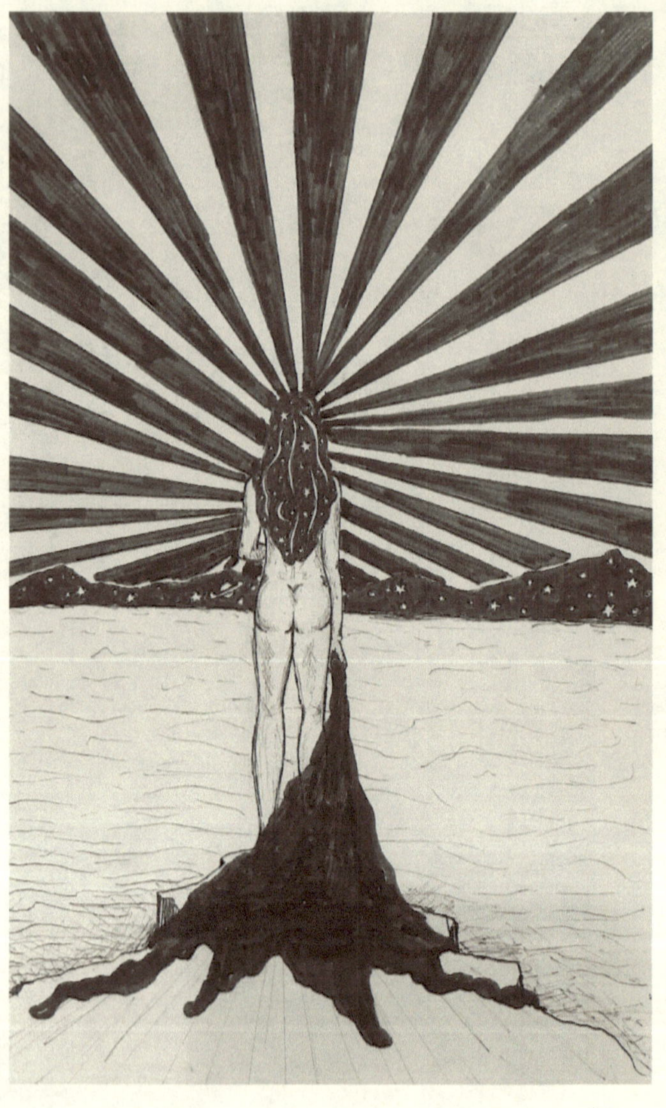

Entomology

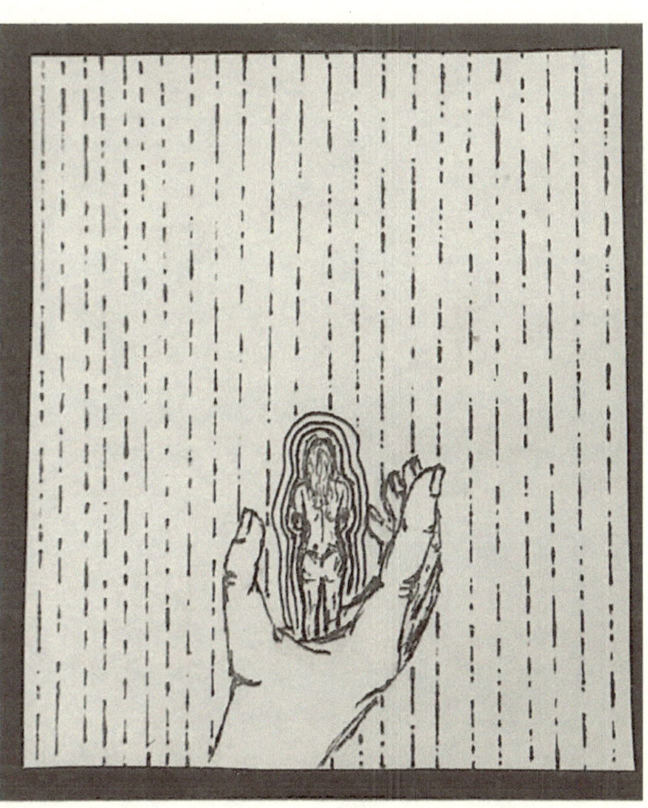

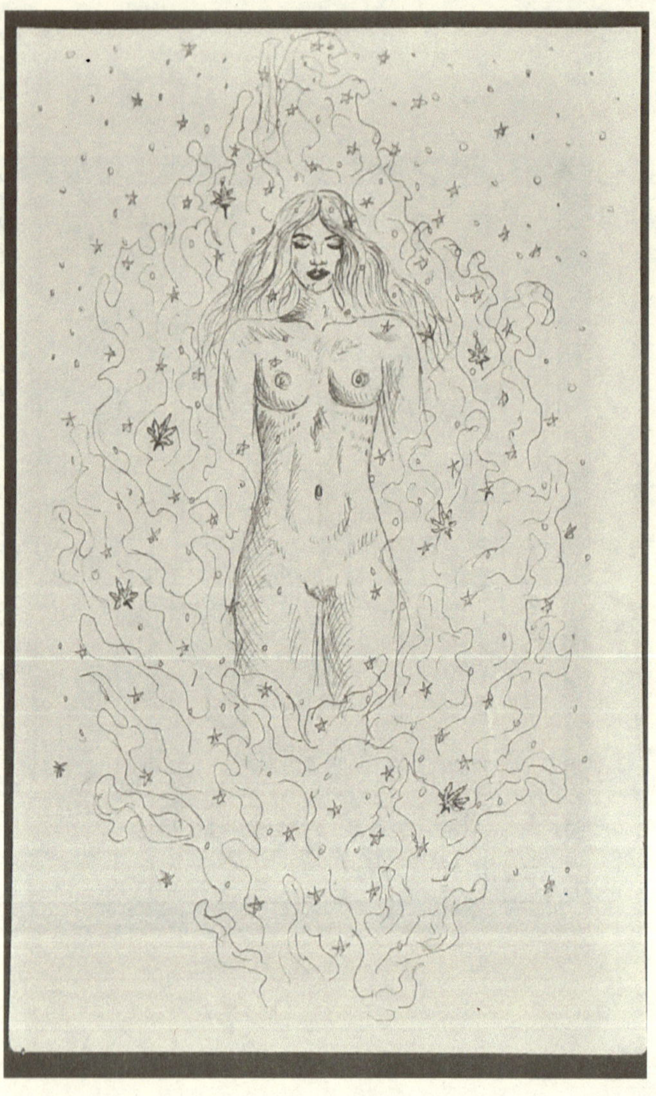

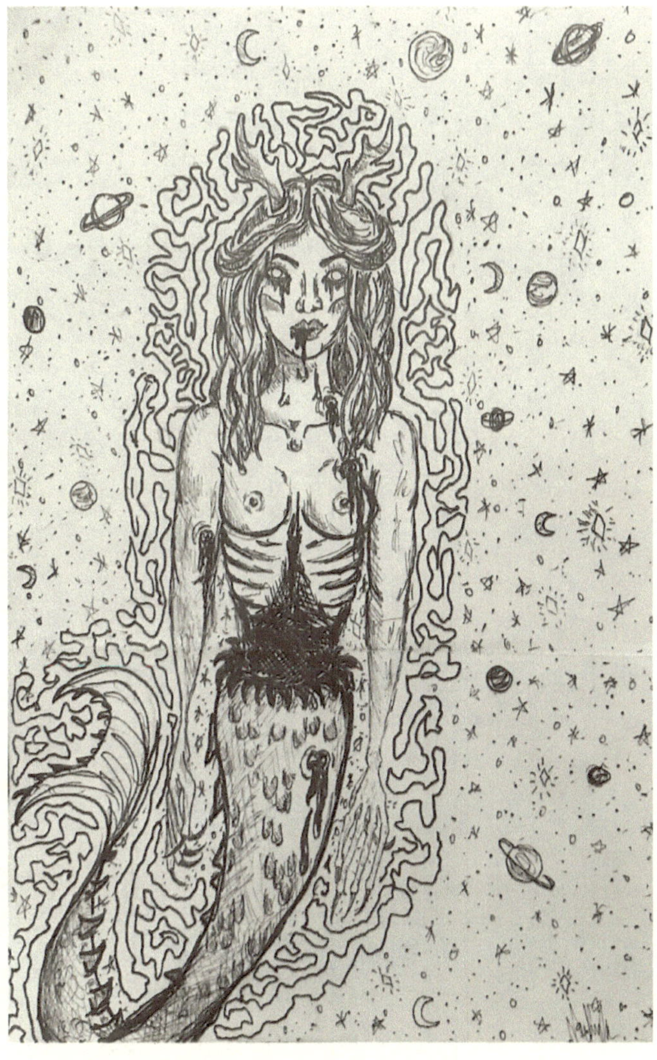

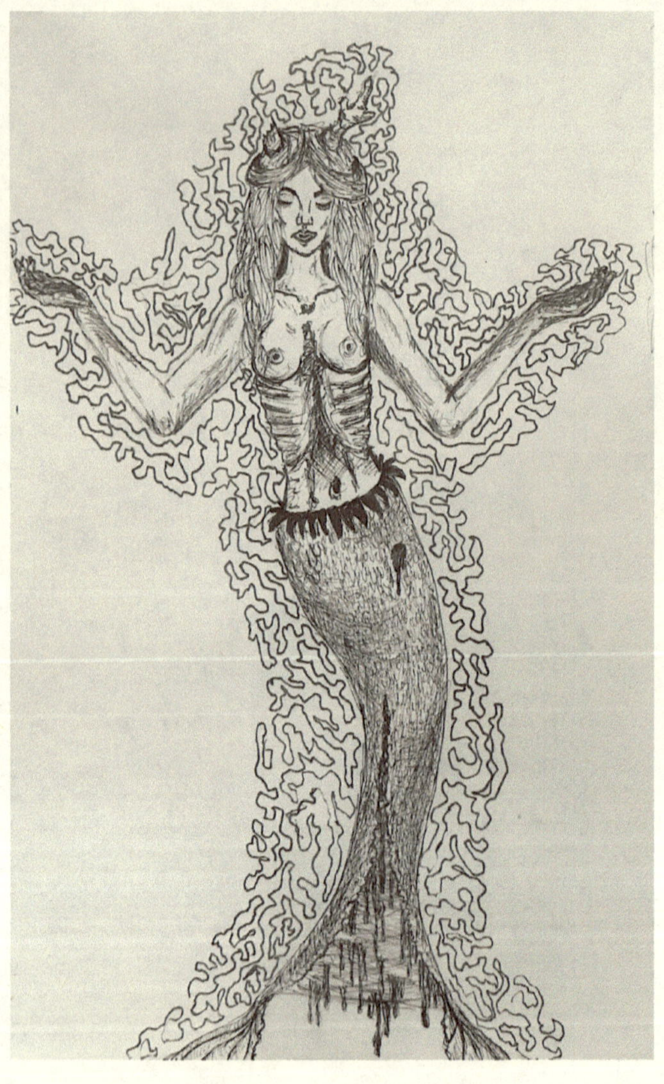

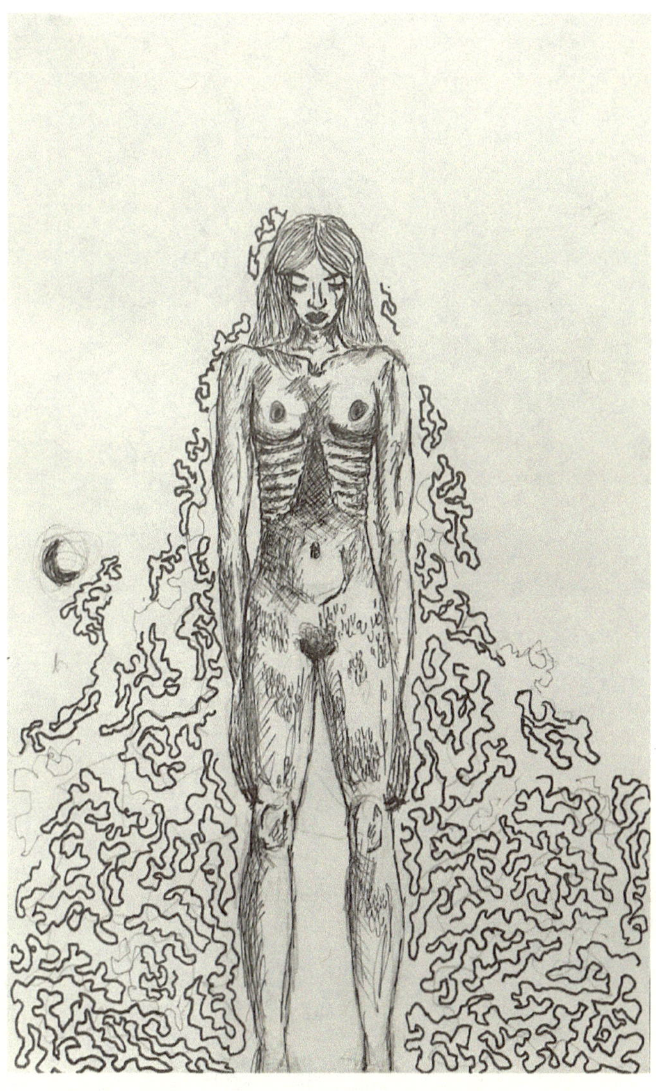

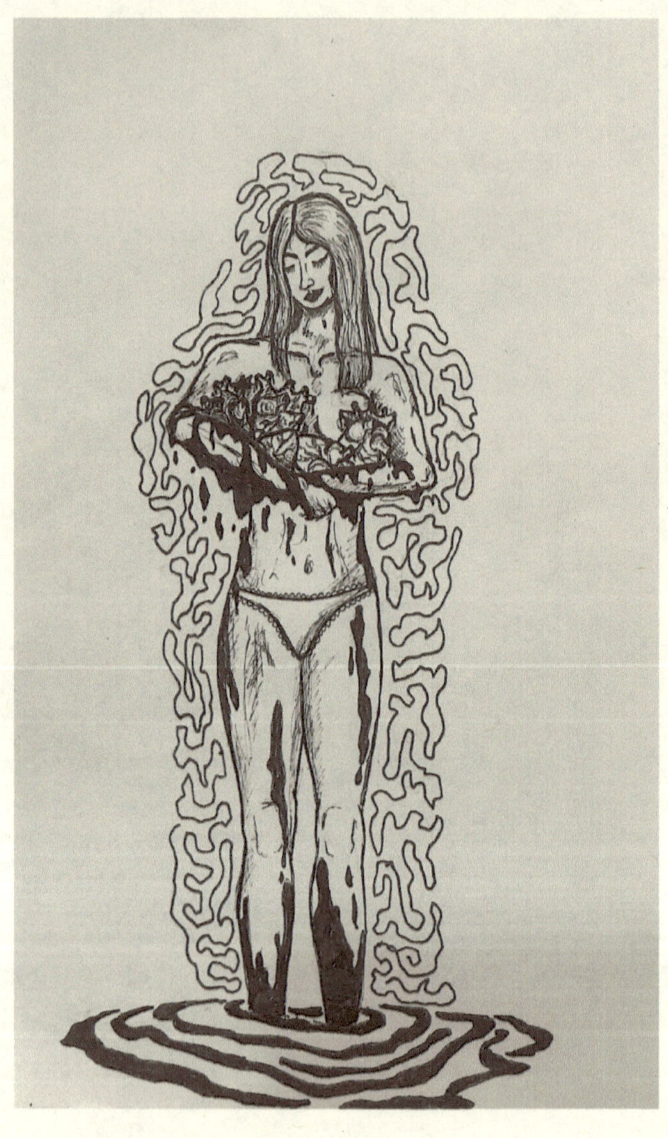

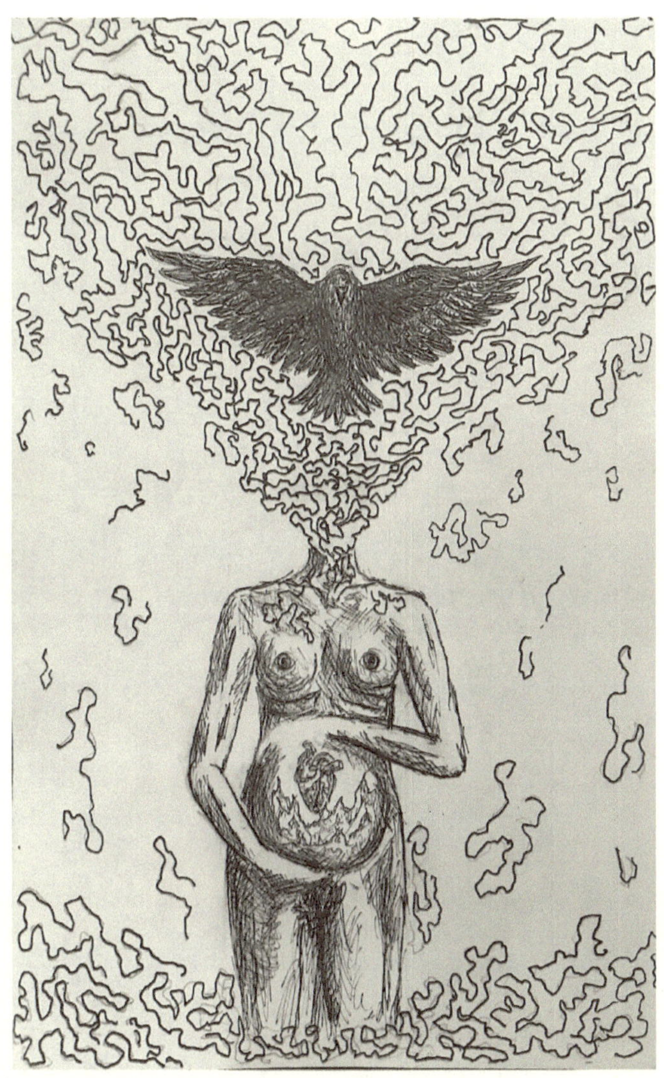

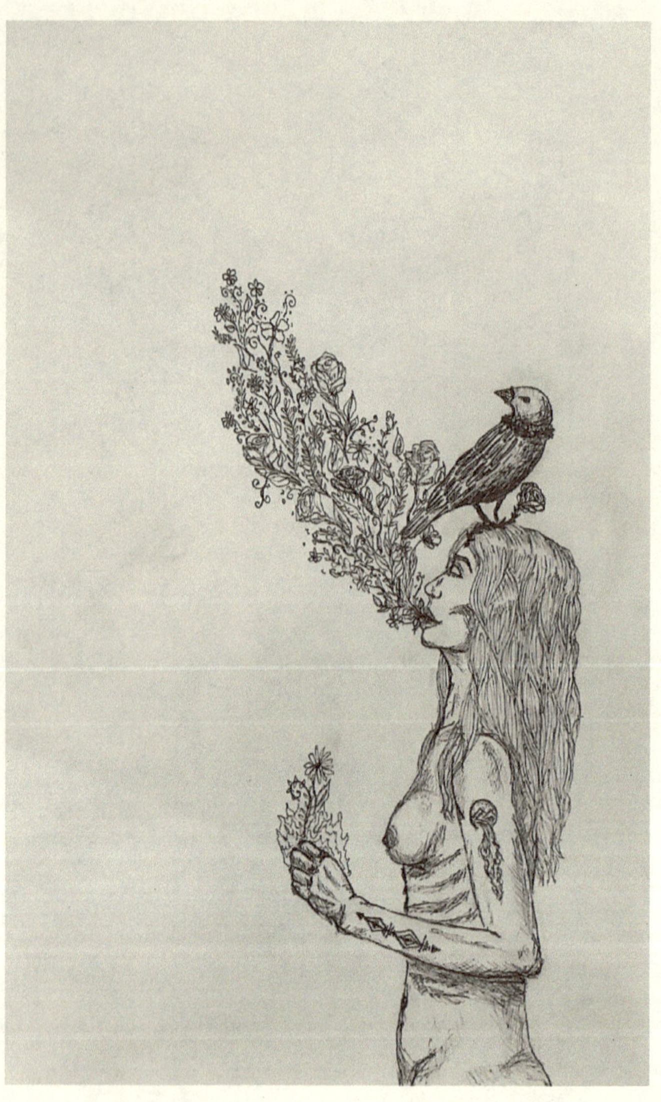

Entomology

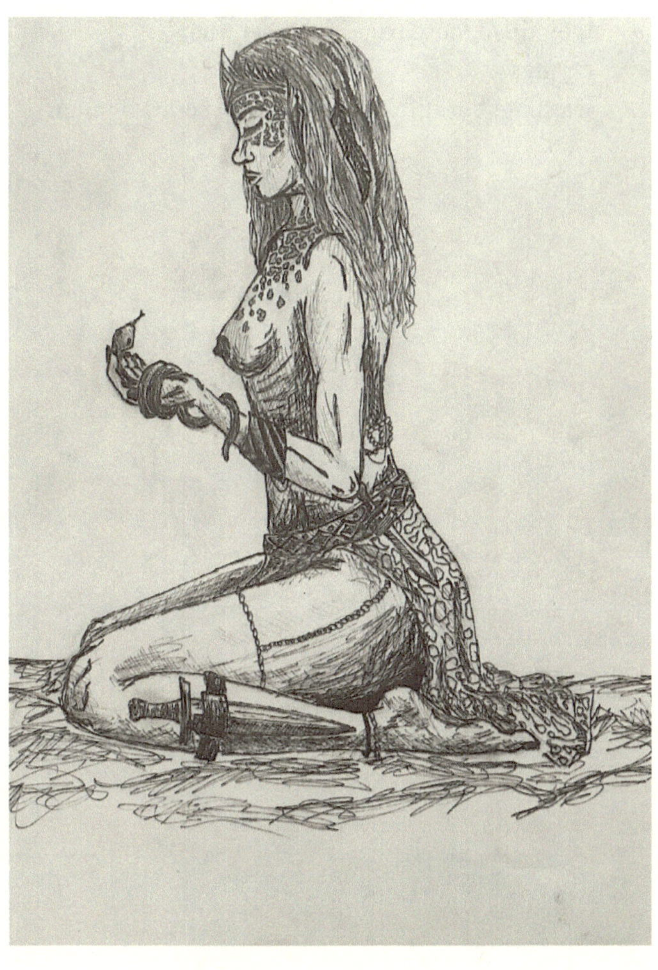

Warning

the words poured
from her ocean eyes and burning hands
they filled those pages with her truths.
crying,
warning: beautiful and broken by her own mind.

Liability

how do you rid yourself,
of countless lies
told every day,
by the passerby?

Stolen

stolen are the sunsets,
full of memories of new love.
stolen are the tall trees,
stuffed with knowledge from above.
stolen are the waves
who leaped, giving earth a shove.
stolen are the gifts,
presented to a soaring dove.
to carry over days, and nights and years,
to deliver to humanity:
tranquility, for all.
stolen,
by our appetite,
a hunger for the fall.

Metempsychosis

a wallowing of cloudless skies
maroon with violet misty greys
fill voids
that were left as footprints
with smells of dying campfires.
and those shallow seaside fumes
swallowed untouched skin.
unspoken words
restless thoughts
and aching hearts.

Thinking chair

what if,
somewhere there is a desert.
stretching for miles and miles
past the sky and earth's core.
and what if in the center,
there sits a plastic chair.
deep blue
with silver legs,
and little screws that catch long hair.
and it is here
that people will come.
to sit
in silence
in a noisy world.
thinking of the things
they wish
they owned,
like memories
of a wild childhood.

The First

my mind murmured
through its desert folds of red volume
yearning for the rain to smother its hungry sands
and my wet mouth spilled words
inconsiderate squalls
into rosebud eyes.
my ivy sprouted thorns as the drought spilled into flash
flood
finally calming the furry within my soul.

Swept

today i swept my soul.
streams of dust billowing
these memories i hold in vain.
collecting them in smokey bags,
delighting in the wind
swooping down and picking up
all these dirty unhappy things.

Spicy Summer

i feel sexy today,
dressed in my favorite lingerie.
nudity empowering
admiring the way
my neck flexes when
my head's thrown back
in laughter and in joy,
messy, wavy, salted hair.
teeth whitened with the sea.
stretch marks singing,
back arching with a stretch,
ass swaying
breasts soaking up the glow.
my painted lips
are singing
i love myself more now, didn't you know?

Manual Labor

i turned every stone on your beach of billowing
hurricanes.
But your mind
was built of boulders and fierce greens,
my blood flowed up your arms
framing the crown, i placed upon your head.
you: my light house of rusted love,
Crumbled at the galaxies in my brain.
i guess i didn't need your light because
I.
Was.
Stardust.

Perpetuation

i wish to etch these memories
into flesh and blood
so, then as mind and body fade like mist
i can hold these vibrant shades
and no tears will fall for youthful exuberant days

Sunrise

the sun traced his touch
down my hair
and shivering skin
through my gentle roses
and silenced eyes.
and the warmth spread a joy that sang
i love myself
into the morning sky

Finally.

this time
it was my own fingers,
weaving pleasure
into pools of twilight.
wrapped in pearly sheets
watching my shadow dance with delight.
whispering,
oh yes!
you're beautiful baby!

Release

goodbye from the midnight light,
of season's long ago.
goodbye from moments wandering,
and gaping at the snow.

goodbye from big dreams,
and small whispers of great sights.
goodbye from tickled waves,
painted crimson in the night.

goodbye from memories far and wide,
slowly lost with every day.
goodbye from strumming strings,
lifting pain away.

goodbye from peaceful, stormy skies,
drenching you with rain.

goodbye from me for now,
from the mind you left behind.

Entomology

ACKNOWLEDGEMENTS

Thank you to those who have come into my life to teach me of love, myself, and empathy. To the firefly's, bumblebee's, and cicada's, thank you for the memories and the lessons; for the support when we loved each other. To my parents, my sister and friends, thank you for your adamant cherishing of me and my creative existence. Thank you for encouraging me to learn loves teachings on my own accord, for being there when things fell apart. Thank you for your support in the process of creating this collection. And thank you most of all to my readers who have let me open my soul and thoughts to them and who cherish the chaos of love as much as I do.

Thank you for all coming with me on the journey through Entomology.

ABOUT THE AUTHOR

McKayla is a 20-year-old philosophy major at Washington State University. She is an avid artist and author who hopes to share her experiences with love and mental illness to inspire readers to embrace life fully with empathy for others and themselves.

www.ingramcontent.com/pod-product-compliance
Lightning Source LLC
La Vergne TN
LVHW051018080826
845145LV00009B/2685

* 9 7 8 0 5 7 8 7 8 2 0 0 3 *